# INDIAN SUBCONTINENT

## ANITA GANERI

**Designer** Steve Prosser
**Text Editor** Belinda Hollyer
**Art Director** Jonathan Hair
**Editor-in-Chief** John C. Miles
**Picture Research** Diana Morris
**Map artwork** Ian Thompson

© 2004 Franklin Watts

First published in 2004
by Franklin Watts
96 Leonard Street
London
EC2A 4XD

Franklin Watts Australia
45-51 Huntley Street
Alexandria
NSW 2015

ISBN 0 7496 5538 0

A CIP catalogue record for this book is
available from the British Library.

Printed in Malaysia

# CONTENTS

# A TROUBLED SUBCONTINENT

**S**ince gaining independence from British rule, the two most powerful countries of the Indian subcontinent, India and Pakistan, have been arch-rivals. This rivalry is fuelled by the fact that, in 1947, the subcontinent was divided along religious lines, resulting in years of hatred, bloodshed and chaos.

## LAND AND PEOPLE

Bordered in the north by mountains, and fringed by the Indian Ocean and Arabian Sea, the vast Indian subcontinent covers about four million square kilometres of southern Asia. The subcontinent is dominated by India, but it also includes Pakistan, Bangladesh, Nepal, Bhutan and Sri Lanka. This huge region has a varied landscape, from the snow-capped Himalayas in the north to dry, sandy desert in the north-west, and lush, tropical rainforest in the south. Within its borders lives at least one-fifth of the world's population. They speak hundreds of different languages, and form an extraordinary mosaic of traditions, cultures and religions.

*The state of Kashmir lies in the northernmost part of the Indian subcontinent. The scenery is breathtaking.*

Strong religious beliefs are a major factor in the region. More than three-quarters of Indians are Hindus and about one-tenth are Muslims. Islam is the state religion of Pakistan and Bangladesh, and the very reason for their independent existence.

## INDEPENDENCE AND AFTER

Although Pakistan and Bangladesh are separate countries today, they were part of British-ruled India until 1947. Then the country was partitioned, into (mainly Hindu) India and (mainly Muslim) Pakistan. At that time, Bangladesh was called East

Pakistan, and Pakistan was called West Pakistan. Bloodshed and chaos followed the partition; millions of people were displaced. Many refugees were massacred as they tried to flee from one new country to another. Conflict in the region continued: in 1971 East Pakistan, with India's help, fought a war with West Pakistan and became the independent republic of Bangladesh.

The painful legacy of 1947 is still apparent at the beginning of the 21st century. At Partition, the Hindu ruler of the state of Kashmir chose to join India, although Kashmir had a mainly Muslim population. His choice was never recognised by Pakistan, and India and Pakistan have fought two wars over Kashmir. Today India and Pakistan both have nuclear weapons. There is real fear that a further incident between them - even a minor one - could set off nuclear war.

## FACT FILE: INDIA

**Full country name:** Republic of India
**Area:** 3,287,590 sq km
**Population:** Over 1 billion
**Capital city:** New Delhi
**Official languages:** Hindi, English
**Major religions:** Hindu 83%; Muslim 11%; Sikh 2%; Christian 2%; other 2%
**Government:** Federal republic

## FACT FILE: PAKISTAN

**Full country name:** Islamic Republic of Pakistan
**Area:** 803,940 sq km
**Population:** 144 million
**Capital city:** Islamabad
**Official language:** Urdu
**Major religions:** Muslim 97%; Hindu and Christian 3%
**Government:** Federal republic

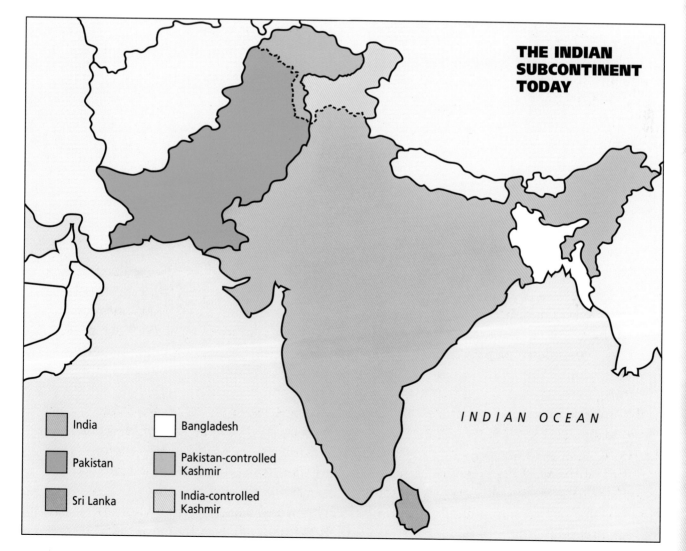

THE INDIAN SUBCONTINENT TODAY

INDIAN OCEAN

India

Pakistan

Sri Lanka

Bangladesh

Pakistan-controlled Kashmir

India-controlled Kashmir

# EARLY HISTORY

**F**or thousands of years, the modern-day countries of India, Pakistan and Bangladesh were one country – simply called 'India' – with a shared history. From the ancient Indus civilisation to the British Raj, it has been a turbulent story. The region was invaded and ruled by many different groups and powers. Each one left its influence behind, adding to the region's dazzling mixture of people and cultures.

## INDUS VALLEY CIVILISATION

India's first major civilisation flourished along the Indus River valley (in modern Pakistan) from about 2500 BC. It centred on the two great cities of Harappa and Mohenjo Daro, and was based on trade in the agricultural produce grown on the fertile river plains.

The Indus Valley civilisation was highly organised. It was ruled by priests rather than kings, and many clay figures of gods and goddesses have been found among the ruins of the Indus cities. These suggest that people worshipped deities similar to those of the later Hindu religion.

## THE VEDIC PERIOD

In about 1500 BC, groups of Indo-Europeans, known as Aryans, began to arrive in north-west India from Central Asia. They spread through the Indus Valley, then pushed east towards the valley of the River Ganges.

*The Indus Valley peoples built the city of Mohenjo Daro, the ruins of which are shown here.*

## HINDUISM

Hinduism is a multi-faceted religion, with different ways of worshipping. However, most Hindus share the same basic beliefs. They believe in a great soul or spirit, called Brahman, who is invisible but is also present in everything. Various aspects of Brahman's power are represented by thousands of Hindu gods and goddesses. Some Hindus worship in *mandirs* (temples); others at small shrines in the home. Hindus believe in reincarnation and in a cycle of birth, death and rebirth. By living a good life, Hindus hope to escape from this cycle and reach *moksha*, or freedom, when a Hindu's soul finally joins with Brahman.

*A picture of the great Hindu god, Brahma.*

The Indo-Europeans brought their own religion with them, which mingled with the beliefs of the Indus Valley peoples to form the basis of Hinduism.

The time of the Aryans is called the Vedic Age. The name comes from collections of sacred hymns called the Vedas, which expressed the Aryans' religious beliefs. At first the Vedas were passed on by word of mouth, and only written down later on. The most important collection is the Rig Veda, which contains more than a thousand hymns recited by priests at ceremonies and sacrifices. The Rig Veda is still one of the most sacred texts of the Hindu religion.

## THE CLASSICAL AGE

During the third century BC, much of India was conquered by the great emperor, Ashoka (ruled 269-231 BC). After a particularly bloody battle, Ashoka converted to Buddhism, which stresses the principle of non-violence. Ashoka sent missionaries far and wide to spread the teachings of the Buddha. After Ashoka's death, his empire collapsed and India split into many different kingdoms.

In about 320 BC, Chandra Gupta I founded the Gupta Empire in north India. This is often called the Classical Age of India. The arts and sciences flourished, and Hinduism replaced Buddhism as India's major religion.

**EARLY HISTORY**

**c2500 BC** The Indus Valley civilisation flourishes along the Indus River valley in modern-day Pakistan

**c2000 BC** The Indus Valley civilisation begins to collapse

**c1500 BC** The Aryans begin to arrive in north-west India;

Their religion forms the basis of Hinduism; this is called the Vedic Age

**c560 BC** The Buddha is born in Nepal

**c321 BC** Chandragupta Maurya founds the Mauryan Empire

**269 BC** Ashoka Maurya comes to the throne

**260 BC** Ashoka converts to Buddhism; he sends missionaries around India and beyond to spread the Buddha's teachings

**231 BC** Ashoka dies. The empire soon starts to collapse

**AD 320** Chandra Gupta I founds the Gupta Empire; the empire lasts until AD 550. This is called the Classical Age of India

**AD 380-415** Reign of Chandra Gupta II, the greatest of the Gupta emperors

# INDIA UNDER MUSLIM RULE

**F**rom AD 1001 a new religion – Islam – arrived in India. Over the next 25 years, Mahmud of Ghazni led a series of raids from Afghanistan into north-west India. His aim was to spread the word of Islam and to plunder the wealth of the Hindu temples. This marked the beginning of 700 years of Muslim rule in India.

## THE DELHI SULTANATE

When Mahmud of Ghazni died in 1030, his successors set out to conquer north-west India. Within 30 years, they controlled most of the Indus and Ganges valleys. In 1206 the first sultan (ruler) of Delhi was proclaimed. By 1236, the Delhi Sultanate, a Muslim kingdom, had become the greatest power in northern India.

From the end of the 14th century, the Sultanate's power declined. In 1398, Delhi was ransacked by the armies of Timur, a Central Asian chieftain. The Sultanate never recovered. In 1526, the last Delhi sultan was defeated in battle, and killed by Babur, the ruler of Kabul in Afghanistan.

## THE MUGHAL EMPIRE

Babur's victory marked the beginning of the Mughal Empire in India. Babur (ruled 1526-1530) was the first of six great Mughal emperors, who established one of the most splendid empires ever seen. It was famous for its buildings, gardens, art and for the grandeur of its courts. At its height, it controlled most of India. The third emperor, Akbar (ruled 1556-1605), is considered the greatest of them all. He was famous for his religious tolerance. Akbar realised that Hindus and other non-Muslims must be treated fairly if Muslim Mughal rule was to succeed. Akbar abolished the hated tax on non-Muslims imposed by the Delhi Sultanate, employed many Hindus at his court, and allowed

### ISLAM

Islam was first taught by the Prophet Muhammad who was born in Makkah, Arabia (now Saudi Arabia) in AD 570. In a series of revelations, Muhammad received the message of Islam from Allah (God). This was later written down in the Qur'an, the holy book of Islam. Followers of Islam are called Muslims. They believe that Allah is the one true God who created the world and everything in it. Within a few years of Muhammad's death, most of Arabia had been converted to Islam. Within a few centuries, Islam had spread west to Spain and North Africa, and east to Turkey, Persia and India.

*This 16th-century painting shows subjects making offerings to the Mughal emperor, Akbar.*

INDIA

*The Taj Mahal, in Agra, was built by the Mughal emperor, Shah Jahan, as a memorial to his wife.*

Hindus who had been forced to convert to Islam to return to their own religion.

## END OF THE EMPIRE

Under Aurangzeb, the last of the great Mughals, the empire reached its largest size. But his rule also signalled the beginning of the end. A strict Muslim, Aurangzeb abandoned Akbar's ideas of religious tolerance. He re-introduced the tax on non-Muslims, imposed *shari'ah* (Muslim law) and destroyed many Hindu temples. Aurangzeb died in 1707, and soon afterwards the empire began to fall apart. The emperor lost authority, and the government was weakened by failing resources and in-fighting.

Mughal emperors remained until 1857, but ruled in name only. In 1858, the British finally exiled the last Mughal emperor.

**INDIA UNDER MUSLIM RULE**

**AD 1001** Mahmud of Ghazni raids north-west India and spreads Islam

**1206** The Delhi Sultanate is founded by Qutb-ud-Din

**1398** Timur attacks Delhi; the sultanate begins to collapse

**1526** The Battle of Panipat; Babur defeats the last Delhi sultan, marking the start of the Mughal Empire

**1526-1530** Reign of Babur, the first great Mughal emperor

**1530-1540** First part of Humayun's reign

**1540-1555** The Sur Dynasty defeats Humayun and rules India

**1555-1556** Second part of Humayun's reign

**1556-1605** Reign of Akbar the Great

**1605-1627** Reign of Jahangir

**1628-1657** Reign of Shah Jahan

**1658-1707** Reign of Aurangzeb, the last of the Great Mughals

**1858** The last Mughal emperor, Bahadur Shah, is exiled by the British

13

# THE EUROPEANS ARRIVE

**F**rom the 15th century, European merchants began to arrive in India to trade in spices, silk, cotton and precious stones. When Mughal power declined, the Europeans were able to increase their influence. Gradually, their attention turned from trade to land and politics. From then on, most of the Indian subcontinent was ruled by Europeans until it gained independence in 1947.

## FOREIGN POWERS

The first Europeans to make their mark on India were the Portuguese. In 1498, the Portuguese navigator, Vasco da Gama, was the first European to reach India by sea, landing at Calicut on the west coast. Further expeditions followed, and for the next 100 years, Portugal controlled trade routes across the Indian Ocean.

In the early 17th century, the Portuguese were joined by the Dutch and English. Each country set up an East India Company to trade in India and south-east Asia.

The Dutch concentrated on the south-east Asian spice trade, but the English sought trading opportunities in India.

## EAST INDIA COMPANY

The first English trading post was set up at Surat, on the west coast, in 1612. By 1690, the East India Company had extended its influence and established bases in, for example, Calcutta (today called Kolkata) and Bombay (today called Mumbai).

In 1756, the new nawab (ruler) of Bengal challenged British power by marching into Calcutta. The British sent Robert Clive to recapture the city. Clive defeated the nawab's army in 1757. The East India Company effectively became the ruler of Bengal province, and increased its grip on India.

'A great prince was dependent on my pleasure. An opulent city lay at my mercy. Its richest bankers bid against one another for my smiles. I walked through vaults which were thrown open to me alone, piled on either side with gold and jewels.'

Robert Clive

*Portuguese navigator, Vasco da Gama.*

## THE 1857 UPRISING

As the East India Company's power grew, so too did resentment among the local people. In 1857 the Company's army was largely made up of Indian soldiers, called sepoys. The cartridges for their muskets had to have the tips bitten off before the bullets inside could fire. A rumour spread that a new issue of cartridges had been greased with beef fat (which Hindus will not touch because they believe cows are sacred) or pork fat (which Muslims will not touch because they believe pigs are unclean). The sepoys refused to use the guns, and mutinied when they were forced to. The rebellion spread across northern India, but eventually it was suppressed and the British took control again.

*This picture shows the scene in the Indian capital, Delhi, when Queen Victoria was officially proclaimed Empress of India on 1 January 1877.*

## BRITISH RULE

The 1857 rebellion marked a turning point in British involvement in India. The dismayed British government decided that the East India Company could no longer be trusted to run its own affairs.

In 1858 the Company was abolished, and the British government took direct control of India. The British Raj (rule) had begun, and a viceroy (governor) was appointed to represent the Crown. In 1877, Queen Victoria was proclaimed Empress of India.

**THE EUROPEANS ARRIVE**

**1498** Vasco da Gama, a Portuguese navigator, becomes the first European to reach India by sea

**1612** The East India Company sets up its first factory at Surat on the west coast of India

**1690** The East India Company also settles in Calcutta and Bombay

**1720** The French establish a trading post near Madras (today called Chennai)

**1757** Robert Clive defeats the Nawab of Bengal at the Battle of Plassey

**1757-1857** The British East India Company extends its control over India

**1857** The First War of Independence (also called the Indian Mutiny)

**1858** The East India Company is abolished; the British Crown takes direct control of India, marking the beginning of the British Raj

**1877** Queen Victoria is proclaimed Empress of India

# TOWARDS INDEPENDENCE

**F**rom the end of the 19th century, many Indians began to speak out against British rule. A new nationalist movement emerged, led by a group of young, well-educated Indians. They believed that Indians should have a greater say in the running of their own country, and that India should eventually become independent.

## POLITICAL PARTIES

In 1885, the Indian National Congress Party was formed. It fought for equal status for Indians, and for the transfer of power into Indian hands. Congress support came from different religions and regions.

Some Muslims, however, mistrusted the Congress Party. They believed it was a Hindu organisation that put Hindu rights first. In 1906, they formed a political party called the All-India Muslim League. Initially, the League's aim was to safeguard the rights of India's Muslims while remaining loyal to Britain. Gradually, though, the idea of a separate Muslim state began to take shape.

## THE AMRITSAR MASSACRE

Despite British promises of a greater share of power for Indians, very little changed.

*The famous Golden Temple in Amritsar. In 1919, the city was the site of an atrocity when British troops fired on an unarmed crowd.*

Then, in April 1919, an unarmed crowd of about 10,000 men, women and children gathered in a walled garden in Amritsar, Punjab, to celebrate a festival. Mistaking this for a political gathering (which was banned), the British commander ordered his troops to open fire. In the massacre that followed, about 400 people were killed and another 1,200 badly injured. This was a tragic turning point. From then on, Indian political leaders demanded complete independence from Britain. Nothing less would do.

## NON-VIOLENT PROTEST

By this time, a softly spoken lawyer, Mohandas Gandhi (1869-1948), had emerged as the independence movement's greatest leader. Known as *Mahatma*, or 'Great Soul', he urged Indians not to fight the British with force but to use peaceful protest, even if it meant going to a jail. He called this tactic *satyagraha*, or 'truth force'.

After the Amritsar Massacre, Gandhi stepped up his campaign. He asked Indians to boycott British goods, refuse to pay taxes and avoid British schools, law courts and government services. In 1930, Gandhi led hundreds of followers on a 400-kilometre march to the sea. There they illegally made salt from seawater, in protest against the unfair government tax on salt, essential for health in India's hot climate.

## MOHANDAS GANDHI

Mohandas Karamchand Gandhi was born in Gujarat in western India on 2 October 1869. He trained as a lawyer in England, then spent 20 years in South Africa where he was shocked at how badly Indian workers were treated. He led the non-violent struggle for their civil rights. Back home again in India, Gandhi became one of the greatest leaders of the Indian independence movement, and began a long campaign of non-violent protest against the British. Gandhi became known as *Mahatma*, or 'Great Soul', and many people around the world were inspired by him. On 30 January 1948, he was assassinated by a Hindu extremist.

**TOWARDS INDEPENDENCE**

**2 October 1869** Mohandas Karamchand Gandhi is born in Porbandar, Gujarat

**1885** The Indian National Congress is formed in Bombay

**1888** Gandhi begins his law studies in England

**1893-1914** Gandhi leads the struggle for civil rights for Indian workers in South Africa

**1906** The All-India Muslim League is formed in Dhaka

**1919** The Amritsar Massacre. Hundreds of innocent people

are killed and injured when troops open fire on the crowd

**1914-18** World War I

**1915** Gandhi returns to India from South Africa

**1920** Gandhi launches his campaign of non-violent, non-cooperation against the British

**1930** Gandhi leads hundreds of followers on his famous Salt March

17

# TOWARDS PARTITION

In 1905, Britain had ordered the division of the eastern province of Bengal into Hindu and Muslim parts. The division was badly managed, and the people of Bengal were outraged because they had not been consulted. Widespread violence and looting followed, with a mass boycott of British goods. The decision was reversed a year later, but Bengal did not stay unified for long.

## QUIT INDIA

The Government of India Act of 1935 created a new constitution for India. It gave Indians a greater say in government and more power to the regions. But many Indian demands were not met, and the British viceroy still had overall control. The situation was tense and dangerous.

Matters came to a head during World War II (1939-45). Millions of Indians fought for Britain, which promised independence after the war. When those promises were not kept, Gandhi launched the 'Quit India' campaign. The British immediately jailed all the Congress Party leaders, including Gandhi and Nehru. But that did not prevent rioting, strikes and protests which broke out all over India, and threatened British rule.

### JAWAHARLAL NEHRU

With his father, Motilal, Jawaharlal Nehru (1889-1964) was one of the leading lights of the Congress Party and became Gandhi's greatest follower. Jawaharlal was born into a well-to-do, upper-class Hindu family whose ancestors came from Kashmir. His father sent him to school and university in England where he studied science and law. On his return to India, he joined his father's law firm but soon became heavily involved in the independence movement. In 1929, he succeeded his father as Congress president.

## TWO NATIONS

Meanwhile, the Muslim League had become more politically active. In 1934, the brilliant lawyer Muhammad Ali Jinnah, a former Congress leader, was elected leader of the Muslim League. The rift between Congress and the Muslim League continued to widen. The League was afraid that, in an independent India, Muslims

*Jawaharlal Nehru (left) and Muhammad Ali Jinnah photographed together in 1946.*

*Rioting in 1946-47 caused major damage to many Indian cities, as shown here at Amritsar.*

would be dominated by Hindus. In 1940, at a meeting of the League in Lahore, Jinnah demanded that a separate, Muslim, state be carved out of India. A name had even been thought up for this new country - Pakistan, which means 'land of the pure' in the Urdu language. 'I will have India divided, or India destroyed,' Jinnah announced. Gandhi, a firm believer in Muslim-Hindu unity, was appalled at the idea of division.

## COMMUNAL RIOTING

By the end of World War II, it was clear that Britain could not stop the nationalist unrest, or keep ruling India for much longer.

The Congress leaders were released from prison and took part in talks with the British government. Despite many discussions, Congress and the Muslim League could not settle their differences. In a show of strength, the League declared a Direct Action Day.

Protesters took to the streets, calling for an independent Pakistan. The result was a bloodbath. During three days of mayhem in Calcutta alone, about four thousand Hindus, Muslims and Sikhs were murdered.

**TOWARDS PARTITION**

**1905** Britain divides the state of Bengal into Hindu and Muslim parts

**1906** After widespread violence and protest, Bengal is re-unified

**1929** Jawaharlal Nehru becomes president of the Congress Party

**1934** Muhammad Ali Jinnah is elected leader of the All-India Muslim League

**1935** The Government of India Act creates a new constitution for India with a greater say for Indians

**1939-1945** World War II

**1940** Jinnah demands that part of India becomes a separate state for Muslims

**1942** Gandhi launches the 'Quit India' campaign to

force the British to leave India; over 60,000 Indians are arrested

**16 August 1946** The Muslim League's Direct Action Day; it is followed by the 'Calcutta killings'

# INDEPENDENCE

**R**ioting quickly spread from Calcutta to India's other big cities in 1946-47. With the violence threatening to escalate out of control, the British chose a drastic solution. They decided to grant independence, and divide the country into Hindu India and Muslim Pakistan.

## THE MOUNTBATTEN PLAN

In March 1947, Lord Mountbatten (1900-79) was appointed as the last viceroy of India, with instructions to oversee the transfer of power within a year. But after talks with Congress and the Muslim League, he decided it was too dangerous to wait. The only way to stop the violence, Mountbatten felt, was to bring forward the date of independence, and to partition India. On 14 July 1947, the British parliament passed the Indian Independence Act. Within a month, India would be divided into two separate nations.

## DRAWING UP BORDERS

Once the decision had been taken to partition India, new borders were needed.

*Jubilant crowds line the streets of New Delhi to shake hands with Lord and Lady Mountbatten on 15 August 1947, India's first full day of independence.*

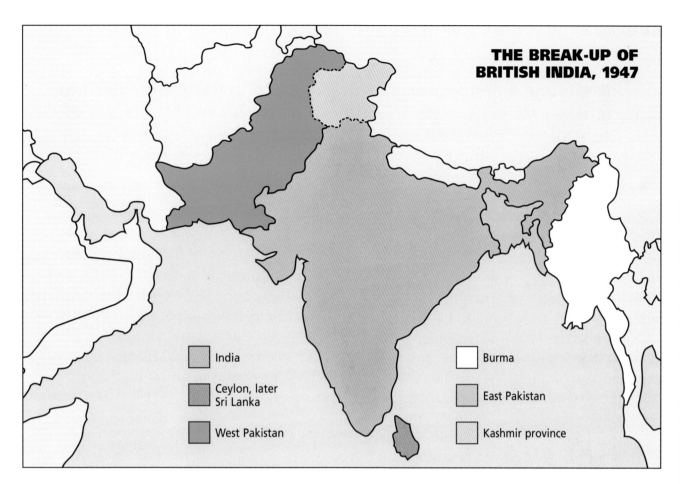

**THE BREAK-UP OF BRITISH INDIA, 1947**

- India
- Ceylon, later Sri Lanka
- West Pakistan
- Burma
- East Pakistan
- Kashmir province

But where exactly should the borders be established? A plan was hastily drawn up. The states of Punjab in the west, and Bengal in the east, would be divided along religious lines. That would leave areas with a Muslim majority in Pakistan, and those with a Hindu majority in India.

Throughout the summer, India's assets were also divided. The military were reorganised into two new armies. But it was impossible to slice the country neatly into Hindu and Muslim parts. The two mainly Muslim areas (renamed West and East Pakistan) were on opposite sides of the country, and separated by more than 1,600 kilometres of Indian territory.

## INDEPENDENCE DAY

For Mahatma Gandhi, achieving India's longed-for freedom only through Partition was a tragedy. But while Gandhi bitterly opposed Mountbatten's plan, Jinnah considered that Partition was a necessity. Nehru also reluctantly agreed to it.

Jinnah celebrated Pakistan's independence. In Karachi on 14 August he was appointed as the first governor-general of the new country, and given the title *Qaid-I-Azam*, or 'great leader'. Despite a bomb scare, Mountbatten went to Karachi to attend the ceremonies that marked this occasion. Then he flew straight to Delhi to take part in the Indian celebrations.

At midnight on 14-15 August, Jawaharlal Nehru gave an historic speech to the Indian parliament. In it, he spoke movingly of India's destiny being fulfilled. Next day, Nehru was sworn in as the first prime minister of independent India. A cheering crowd of about half a million people watched as the new flag of a free India was raised. But the celebrations did not last for long.

# BLOODBATH

**I**ndia and Pakistan were free at last, but there was a terrible price to pay for independence. Partition was followed by a bloodbath. As millions of terrified people fled across the new borders, about half a million Hindus, Muslims and Sikhs were massacred.

## CHAOS AND DIVISION

Some areas of India were mainly Hindu or Muslim, but others were more evenly mixed. When the new borders were announced, millions of people were stranded in the 'wrong' country. In fear of their lives, they left the homes in which they had lived for generations and fled to the other side. For months, particularly in the Punjab, Muslims who found themselves in India fled to Pakistan. Hindus and Sikhs who found themselves in Pakistan fled to India.

In the violence that followed, trainloads of Muslims fleeing west were held up and killed by Hindu and Sikh mobs. Hindus and Sikhs fleeing east suffered the same fate at the hands of Muslim mobs. Millions of refugees poured into India from Pakistan, and refugee camps in Delhi were soon overflowing with

*Following partition, millions of refugees fled to safety. Muslims went to Pakistan, Hindus and Sikhs to India.*

*Police use tear gas to disperse crowds during the riots in Calcutta, 17 December 1947.*

terrified, starving people. In the filthy conditions, deadly diseases such as cholera and typhoid spread rapidly.

## ECONOMIC CHAOS

Partition also brought economic disaster. Pakistan, for example, was left short of office workers and administrators - jobs previously held by Hindus. Raw materials from Pakistan were cut off from the factories in India where they were usually processed. In Bengal, Calcutta (India) had the region's jute mills and port. However, the jute itself was grown in East Bengal (East Pakistan) which had no jute mills to work it.

## GANDHI'S DESPAIR

Gandhi's pleas for tolerance failed to stop the violence in Calcutta, and he took drastic personal action. If the violence did not end, he was prepared to fast until he died. In September 1947, both sides were shamed by him into an uneasy peace. In January 1948, Gandhi began another fast, this time in Delhi, where the worst riots in the city's

> *'I cannot live while hatred and killing mar the atmosphere... I therefore plead with you to give up the present madness.'*
>
> **Mahatma Gandhi**

history had broken out. Again, it worked. But some Hindus remained suspicious of Gandhi and his tolerance of Muslims. On 30 January Gandhi was on his way to a prayer meeting when a Hindu fanatic shot him dead.

In a radio broadcast, Nehru said: 'The light has gone out of our lives and there is darkness everywhere. I do not know what to tell you and how to say it. Our beloved leader, *Bapu* as we called him, the Father of the Nation, is no more.'

# WAR IN KASHMIR

**A**fter independence, the 562 'princely states' ruled by Indian maharajas and princes were given the choice of joining either India or Pakistan. For most, the decision was reasonably clear cut, based on geography and the religion of their people. Kashmir, however, faced a dreadful dilemma.

*A scene on the Dal Lake in Srinagar, Kashmir.*

## KASHMIR

The beautiful region of Kashmir lies in the foothills of the Himalayas, in the far north of the subcontinent. During the British Raj, it was famous as a summer holiday retreat away from the heat of the plains.

After Partition, Kashmir's ruler faced an agonising decision. Geographically, Kashmir had borders with both India and Pakistan. Religiously, the majority of its people were Muslims, although its ruler was Hindu.

For months, the maharaja of Kashmir could not decide which country to join. Then events took place that forced a decision.

## REACHING A DECISION

In October 1947, groups of Pashtun tribesmen from Pakistan's north-west frontier province invaded Kashmir. Spurred on by reports of violence against Kashmir's Muslims and supported by Pakistan, they headed for the capital, Srinagar, intent on taking Kashmir for Pakistan. Faced with a breakdown of law and order, the panic-stricken maharaja finally made up his mind. In return for military help, he agreed that Kashmir should join India.

Immediately, Indian planes began to airlift troops into Srinagar to repel the invasion. Pakistan, meanwhile, refused to accept the maharaja's decision. It claimed that India had forced his hand, and that the document he had signed was fraudulent. More fighters poured into Kashmir from Pakistan. The first Indo-Pak War had begun.

**Indian soldiers in Kashmir take a prisoner during the 1947 fighting.**

> *'In the opinion of the government of Pakistan, the accession of Kashmir is based on fraud and violence and as such cannot be recognised.'*
>
> **Government of Pakistan official statement, 30 October 1947**

## RELUCTANT CEASEFIRE

On 1 January 1949, after months of bitter fighting, the two sides finally agreed a ceasefire, helped by the United Nations (UN). A ceasefire line was drawn across Kashmir. One-third of the state was awarded to Pakistan; the rest went to India.

Neither side was satisfied. Pakistan claimed Kashmir because of geographical closeness, and because its people were mainly Muslim. It also accused India of breaking its promise of a referendum, so Kashmiris could decide their own fate. India claimed that Kashmir had been freely signed over by the maharaja, and refused to give any part of it up. This conflict brought the two countries to the brink of war many more times.

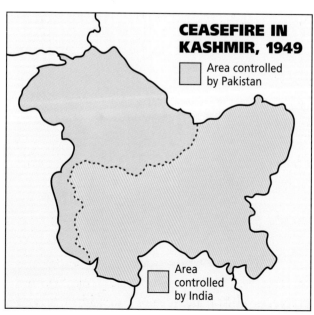

**CEASEFIRE IN KASHMIR, 1949**

Area controlled by Pakistan

Area controlled by India

# THE NEHRU ERA IN INDIA

In August 1947, Jawaharlal Nehru became the first prime minister of an independent India. After years of struggle against the British, and many years in jail as a political prisoner, his dream to see his country free had finally come true.

## NEHRU'S CAREER

On 26 January 1950, India adopted a new constitution and became a republic with a parliamentary government. The country's first general election was held in 1951-52. Now that 173 million Indians were qualified to vote, organising the election was a mammoth task. Under Nehru's leadership, the Congress Party won a huge majority of seats and Nehru was re-elected as prime minister. His vision was for a modern, secular India with social justice for everyone, especially the poor.

In 1951, Nehru began a 'Five-Year Plan' to raise India's standard of living. The plan had many successes. Food production and industry increased. The number of children attending school rose, and rights for women, and for farmers, improved.

*Lord Mountbatten (right, in uniform) swears in Nehru as prime minister of India on 15 August 1947.*

> 'If India is split up into two or more parts and can no longer function as a political and economic unit, her progress will be seriously affected. There will be the direct weakening effect, but much worse will be the inner psychological conflict between those who wish to reunite her and those who oppose this.'
>
> Jawaharlal Nehru, from *The Discovery of India*, 1944

*Chinese prime minister, Zhou Enlai, is greeted by Nehru as he makes a state visit to India in 1954. By 1962, the two countries were at war.*

## FOREIGN POLICIES

In foreign affairs, Nehru followed a non-alignment policy, refusing to let India side with either of the world's two rival superpowers - the USSR and the USA. A test of this policy came in October 1962, when a long-standing border dispute with China led to Chinese forces invading north-east India. Embarrassingly, the invasion took the Indian government by surprise and the army was totally unprepared. Nehru was forced to abandon his principles and call on the USA and Britain for help. This badly damaged his reputation.

The dispute over Kashmir continued on throughout the whole of Nehru's time in office. India would not accept the UN's call for a referendum until Pakistan withdrew from Kashmir, and Pakistan refused to do that. With tensions running high, thousands of Indian troops were kept stationed in Kashmir and the Punjab, on full alert.

## DEATH OF NEHRU

Despite the disaster of the war with China, Nehru was a hero to millions of Indian people who called him *Panditji* or 'great teacher'. He was a charismatic figure and statesman, who travelled tirelessly around the world, representing India's interests in his meetings with world leaders. Soon after the Chinese invasion, though, Nehru's health began to fail. A stroke in January 1964 left him confined to a wheelchair.

A few months later, in May 1964, Nehru had another, fatal stroke. More than two million people lined his funeral route through Delhi. The struggle to succeed him as prime minister of India was won by Lal Bahadur Shastri, a quiet, modest man and a member of Nehru's cabinet.

# PAKISTAN'S EARLY YEARS

**M**uhammad Ali Jinnah's dream was realised when Pakistan gained independence in August 1947. But the new country's early years were turbulent. It was immediately plunged into war with India over Kashmir (see pages 24-25), and there were years of political instability and military rule. Serious social and economic problems had to be tackled, together with unrest in East Pakistan.

## QAID-I-AZAM

In August 1947, Jinnah became the first governor general of Pakistan. But the *Qaid-I-Azam*, or 'great leader', did not live long enough to see his new country grow. He died of tuberculosis in September 1948.

Jinnah's deputy was the prime minister, Liaquat Ali Khan (1895-1951). He inherited the task of drawing up a constitution for the new country. Liaquat was a refugee from India, and an experienced politician. A moderate, he wanted Pakistan to become a secular country, ruled by a democratically elected government. But Pakistan's religious leaders demanded an Islamic state, ruled by Muslim law. Liaquat tried to balance the two demands, but was never able to put his ideas into practice. On 16 October 1951,

*'You will find that, in the course of time, Hindus would cease to be Hindus and Muslims would cease to be Muslims, not in the religious sense because that is the personal faith of each individual, but in the political sense as citizens of the state.'*

Jinnah, in his first speech as governor general of Pakistan, 1947

*Liaquat Ali Khan became the leader of Pakistan after Jinnah's death. He was assassinated in 1951.*

he was assassinated by fanatics because of his refusal to wage war on India.

## ISLAMIC REPUBLIC

With both Jinnah and Liaquat gone, Pakistan entered a long period of political instability, during which the country was governed by a series of governor generals and prime ministers. After independence, the Muslim League, which had done so much to create Pakistan, was renamed the All-Pakistan Muslim League. It became the country's main political party but its popularity gradually declined.

The League lost power in East Pakistan in 1954, and then in West Pakistan. In 1956, a new constitution was drawn up to establish Pakistan as an Islamic republic. Under this, Major-General Iskander Mirza became the first president of Pakistan. Two years later, President Mirza cancelled the constitution, banned all political parties and imposed martial (military) law.

*Iskander Mirza (centre left) meets the US vice-president, Richard Nixon (centre right) in 1958.*

## PAKISTAN'S EARLY LEADERS

**HEAD OF STATE
(GOVERNOR GENERAL)**
**1947-48** Mohammad Ali Jinnah
**1948-51** Khwaja Nazimuddin
**1951-55** Ghulam Mohammad
**1955-56** Iskander Mirza

**PRESIDENT**
**1956-58** Iskander Mirza

**PRIME MINISTER**
**1947-51** Liaquat Ali Khan
**1951-53** Khwaja Nazimuddin
**1953-55** Muhammad Ali Bogra
**1955-56** Chaudhry Mohammad Ali
**1956-57** H. S. Suhrawardhi
**1957** I. I. Chundrigar
**1957-58** Malik Firoz Khan Nun

**PAKISTAN'S EARLY YEARS**

**14 August 1947** Pakistan becomes independent, with Jinnah as governor general and Liaquat Ali Khan as prime minister

**11 September 1948** Death of Jinnah

**16 October 1951** Liaquat Ali Khan is assassinated because he refuses to wage war on India

**1954** The All-Pakistan Muslim League loses power in East Pakistan; the pro-independence Awami League gains power

**1956** A new constitution makes Pakistan officially an Islamic republic

**1956** Major-General Iskander Mirza becomes the first president of Pakistan

**1958** President Mirza cancels the constitution, bans all political parties, and declares martial law

**1958** Government is overthrown by the army. General Ayub Khan seizes power and becomes president

# THE GOVERNMENT OF AYUB KHAN

In 1958, General Ayub Khan, the commander-in-chief of the Pakistani army, overthrew the government and took power. He wanted to bring stability to Pakistan and strengthen the economy. President Mirza was exiled to London, and many other politicians were replaced by army officers.

## TROUBLE IN THE EAST

The gulf between West and East Pakistan continued to grow. Since Pakistan's creation, there had been conflict between the two parts of the country. Not only were they divided geographically, they had little culture in common apart from religion. They did not even share the same language. Urdu had been made the official language of Pakistan, but most East Pakistanis spoke Bengali.

There was also resentment about the unfair distribution of wealth. West Pakistan began to prosper under Ayub Khan, while East Pakistan remained the poor relation.

In 1954, the Muslim League was defeated in East Pakistan's elections. The Awami League (People's League) became the country's main political party. Under the leadership of Sheikh Mujibur Rahman (1920-75), the Awami League called for greater freedom for East Pakistan, and for more control over its own affairs.

## WAR AND PEACE

Ayub Khan tried to improve relations with India, but Kashmir remained a flashpoint. Pakistan's growing friendship with the USA and China only added to the tension. In summer 1965, fighting broke out when

*This Kashmiri village was destroyed by Pakistani troops in September 1965.*

*Ayub Khan (centre) and Indian Prime Minister Lal Bahadur Shastri (left) at Tashkent in 1966.*

Pakistani troops entered Indian-held Kashmir, intending to cut Kashmir off from the Indian Punjab. But India's army was much larger than Pakistan's. Soon Indian tanks were rolling across the border towards the city of Lahore. The war lasted barely a month before the UN brought about a ceasefire.

In January 1966, Ayub Khan and Shastri flew to Tashkent in Uzbekistan for talks about Kashmir, and signed the Tashkent Declaration. This was a document that stated that the two countries were resolved to end the conflict peacefully, and to restore normal relations. The declaration, however, marked a downturn in Ayub Khan's political career. His enemies accused him of siding with India, and violent protests broke out. Ill-health and loss of support forced Ayub Khan to resign in 1969. Yahya Khan became president, and imposed martial law again.

## AYUB KHAN

Educated at the Royal Military Academy in Sandhurst, England, Ayub Khan served for many years in the British Indian Army. When India was partitioned, he went to Pakistan and, in 1951, became commander-in-chief of the Pakistani army. With help from the USA, he built up a large army, and became a powerful political figure. Ayub Khan was president of Pakistan from 1958-69. He kept a firm grip on power and quashed opposition groups. During his time in office, the Pakistani economy grew quickly. Ayub Khan lifted martial law in 1962 when a new constitution was drawn up. Among other things, the constitution said that any president of Pakistan must be a Muslim.

# INDIRA GANDHI AND BANGLADESH

**O**n 10 January 1966, Lal Bahadur Shastri died of a heart attack and Indira Gandhi became India's first woman prime minister. Five years later her government supported East Pakistan in its war of independence, causing further tension in the subcontinent.

## BANGLADESH

In December 1970, general elections were held in Pakistan. The Awami League, led by Sheikh Mujib, won a majority of seats in the new national assembly and demanded independence for East Pakistan.

### INDIRA GANDHI

Daughter of Jawaharlal Nehru, Indira Gandhi served four terms of office: 1966-67, 1967-71, 1971-77 and 1980-84. After the 1967 general election, deep divisions appeared in the Congress Party. The Party split into two rival factions – Congress 'O', led by Indira, and Congress 'R' that wanted Indira out. But in the general election of 1971, Indira won a landslide victory, promising to get rid of poverty. In August 1971, she signed a treaty of peace and friendship with the USSR. Most of that year, however, was taken up with the growing tension over East Pakistan. Indira Gandhi was assassinated in 1984 (see page 38).

*Yahya Khan became president of Pakistan in 1969. He resigned after the 1971-72 war.*

President Yahya Khan postponed the first meeting of the new assembly, which caused an outcry. In March 1971, Mujib was arrested and sent to prison in West Pakistan. He called on his followers in East Pakistan to rise up, and the result was nine months of civil war between West and East Pakistan. West Pakistan sent troops into Dhaka (the capital of East Pakistan) and millions of refugees poured across the border into India.

India backed East Pakistan. Indira Gandhi supplied Indian troops, using arms provided by the USSR, to support the East Pakistani freedom fighters. Heavy fighting also broke out along the ceasefire line in Kashmir. On 16 December 1971, the West Pakistani army surrendered and East Pakistan became the independent country of Bangladesh. Sheikh Mujib was released from prison, and flew home in triumph to become Bangladesh's first prime minister.

## SIMLA AGREEMENT

In both India and Bangladesh, Indira Gandhi was hailed as a heroine. For Pakistan, however, the war was a humiliating defeat. Yahya Khan resigned in disgrace and was succeeded by Zulfikar Ali Bhutto (1928-79), leader of the opposition Pakistan's People Party.

In July 1972, Indira Gandhi and Bhutto met for peace talks about Kashmir. The leaders agreed to withdraw their troops and respect a new ceasefire line (similar to the previous line) which would be called the Line of Control. But neither country was prepared to give up their claim to the territory, and so the Kashmir question remained unsettled.

'In Jammu and Kashmir, the line of control resulting from the ceasefire of December 17, 1971 shall be respected by both sides without prejudice to the recognised position of either side. Neither side shall seek to alter it unilaterally, irrespective of mutual differences and legal interpretation. Both sides further undertake to refrain from threat or the use of force in violation of this line.'

Part of the Simla Agreement, July 1972

*Zulfikar Ali Bhutto (left) and Indira Gandhi shake hands in the Indian city of Simla in July 1972.*

# BHUTTO AND PAKISTAN

**A**fter Pakistan's defeat in the civil war and the devastating loss of Bangladesh, Zulfikar Ali Bhutto worked hard to lift his country's spirits and restore its battered pride. A charismatic figure and a powerful speaker, Bhutto served first as president and then as prime minister.

*Bangladeshi prime minister, Sheik Mujib (centre) stands with Pakistani president, Fazal Elahi Ghaudhri (left) and Zulfikar Ali Bhutto on 23 February 1974, when Pakistan finally recognised Bangladesh as an independent country.*

## RISE OF BHUTTO

The son of a politician, Zulfikar Ali Bhutto studied politics and law in the USA and Britain. He returned to Pakistan in 1953 and soon entered politics. Bhutto served as minister of commerce and then foreign minister in Ayub Khan's government. He resigned from the government in 1967 in protest over Pakistan's peace talks with India, and founded his own political party - the Pakistan People's Party (PPP).

After the war with East Pakistan, Yahya Khan handed power over to Bhutto. A year later, Bhutto lifted martial law and promised democracy for Pakistan. In 1973, under the new constitution, he was sworn in as prime minister. His political and diplomatic skills won him the support of many other Islamic countries, including Saudi Arabia and Libya.

## NUCLEAR TESTS

Despite the 1972 Simla Agreement, diplomatic relations with India remained strained. The problem of Kashmir still seemed impossible to solve, although both sides agreed that any future action must be peaceful. In May 1974, however, India held its first nuclear tests in desert close to the border with Pakistan. The Indian prime minister, Indira Gandhi, wrote to Bhutto personally to assure him that Pakistan had nothing to fear. India would only use nuclear energy for peaceful purposes, not for nuclear weapons. Despite this, Pakistan was deeply suspicious of India's intentions. A few years later, Pakistan began to develop its own nuclear programme with support from other Islamic countries and China. Bhutto himself pledged that Pakistan would match India's nuclear power, whatever the cost.

## DOWNFALL AND DEATH

Hoping to strengthen his hold on power, Bhutto called elections for March 1977. His party won by a large majority, but then Bhutto's enemies accused him of rigging the elections. Violent clashes broke out between Bhutto's supporters and his opponents. In July, General Mohammad Zia-ul-Haq, the army chief of staff, seized power in a military coup. Bhutto was arrested and thrown into prison. He was later tried for the murder of a political opponent and sentenced to death. Despite international protests and appeals to spare his life, he was hanged in April 1979.

> '*Pakistan has reasons for special anxiety because of confrontation and unresolved disputes which have bedevilled relations between India and Pakistan... The nuclear explosion is an event which cannot be viewed in isolation from its surrounding circumstances.*'
>
> **Bhutto's reply to a letter from Indira Gandhi, May 1974**

*Bhutto's execution in 1979 caused international outrage. Here, British supporters take part in a demonstration.*

**G**eneral Zia-ul-Haq put Pakistan under martial law once more. In 1978, Zia declared himself president, and tightened the military's hold on the government. He remained head of the country until his death in 1988, and so became the longest-serving leader in Pakistan's history.

## HOME AND ABROAD

At home, President Zia's main goal was to turn Pakistan into a strictly Islamic country. He began to introduce Islamic systems of education, law and government. All Pakistani laws were now based on Islamic law, and Islamic courts were set up to try cases and decide punishments.

At the same time, Zia tried to develop friendlier relations with India. He met members of the Indian government and signed agreements on many issues, including trade and communications. Zia also asked India to sign a treaty to end a

### ZIA-UL-HAQ

Mohammad Zia-ul-Haq was born in the Punjab in 1924. He rose quickly through the ranks of the Pakistani army and, under Bhutto, was promoted to lieutenant-general. In 1976, he was made chief of staff. After seizing power, Zia pledged that new elections would be held. In March 1978, however, he cancelled the elections, banned all political activity, and shut down a number of newspapers. Further elections, promised for 1979, were also cancelled. Fearing opposition from Bhutto's PPP, Zia also banned all political parties. In 1985, he finally announced a return to democracy for Pakistan, allowed elections, and lifted martial law. Most PPP supporters boycotted the elections, claiming that they were rigged. Zia, however, declared the elections a great success and began a new five-year term as president.

possible nuclear arms race, and agree mutual inspection of nuclear sites. But these proposals were never adopted.

The new-found friendliness between the two countries did not last. In 1986, India accused Pakistan of arming and training Sikhs in the Punjab who were fighting for a homeland. Pakistan was alarmed by anti-Muslim riots in India, and Zia accused India of helping his political enemies. Tensions rose further when both sides held military exercises close to their border.

*Mohammad Zia-ul-Haq was the army chief of staff when he seized power from Bhutto.*

## DEATH AND SUCCESSION

In 1988, President Zia suddenly dismissed the prime minister and dissolved parliament. He announced that elections would be held within 90 days, but these were later delayed for several months. Before the elections could take place, however, Zia was killed in a mysterious air crash in the Punjab. An investigation later claimed that the crash was the result of 'a criminal act of sabotage'.

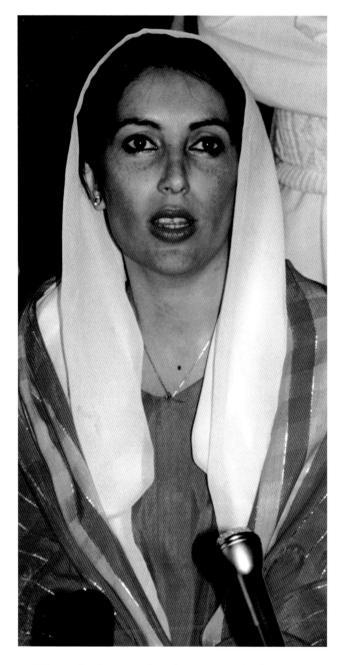

*Zulfikar Ali Bhutto's daughter Benazir Bhutto became prime minister of Pakistan in 1988.*

### BENAZIR BHUTTO

Benazir Bhutto was born in Karachi, Pakistan, in 1953. The daughter of Zulfikar Ali Bhutto, politics were part of Benazir's life from an early age. She was educated in the USA, then studied politics, philosophy and economics at Britain's Oxford University. After her father's execution in 1979, she became head of his party. In 1984, she went into exile in England, returning two years later to lead the party against President Zia. She served two terms as prime minister, from 1988-1990, and from 1993-1996. Then her government was accused of corruption, and dismissed.

In the elections that were held after Zia's death, the opposition PPP (Pakistan People's Party) won a majority. Its leader, Benazir Bhutto - who had been living in exile in Britain - was the daughter of the former Prime Minister, Zulfikar Ali Bhutto.

Since her return from exile she had travelled around the country, drawing large crowds with her speeches, and urging the government to hold elections. On 1 December 1988, Benazir was sworn in as prime minister of Pakistan. She was the first woman to head an elected government in a Muslim country.

### PAKISTAN'S PRIME MINISTERS 1958–

| | |
|---|---|
| 1958-1971 | Ayub Khan |
| 1973-1977 | Zulfikar Ali Bhutto |
| 1977-1985 | Zia-ul-Haq |
| 1985-1988 | Khan Junejo |
| 1988-1990 | Benazir Bhutto |
| 1990-1993 | Nawaz Sharif |
| 1993-1996 | Benazir Bhutto |
| 1996-1999 | Miraj Khalid, Nawaz Sharif |
| 1999- | Pervez Musharraf |

# CONTINUING CONFLICT

**I**n October 1984, Indira Gandhi was assassinated by her Sikh bodyguards. Her elder son, Rajiv (1944-91), succeeded her as head of the Congress Party and prime minister of India. With new, young leaders in India and Pakistan, both from famous political families, it was hoped that relations between the two countries would improve.

## FRIENDLY TALKS

Things started off well. The South Asian Association for Regional Cooperation (SAARC) was launched in 1985, with Gandhi's backing. The group offered south Asian leaders a forum to discuss their problems. In December 1988, Rajiv Gandhi went to Pakistan to attend the annual SAARC conference - the first visit by an Indian prime minister since 1960. His meeting with Benazir Bhutto was hailed as a great success. The two prime ministers got on well. They signed several new agreements, including one that promised neither India nor Pakistan would attack the other's nuclear plants.

*Benazir Bhutto and Rajiv Gandhi pictured together at the SAARC conference in 1988.*

## KASHMIR IN CRISIS

Despite those friendly relations, Kashmir remained a problem. In 1989, a new wave of violence broke out. Many young Kashmiri Muslims in Indian-held Kashmir demanded independence. India accused Pakistan of backing and arming these militant groups, but Pakistan said it was only offering political support.

The situation soon deteriorated. India rushed troops into Kashmir to put down the attacks. As the fighting got worse, foreign journalists were flown out of the country, and tourists were kept away. Hostilities continued throughout the 1990s, and thousands were killed. By 1999, Pakistan-backed forces invaded Indian-held Kashmir, bringing both sides to the brink of war again. A bitter two-month battle along the Line of Control only ended when Pakistan withdrew its troops.

## COMMUNAL VIOLENCE

The early 1990s also saw a rise in violence between Hindus and Muslims in India. The focus of the trouble was a Muslim mosque in the small town of Ayodhya, in northern India. Some Hindus believe that Ayodhya is the birthplace of Lord Rama, one of the most important Hindu gods. They claimed that the mosque was built on the site of an ancient Hindu temple, dedicated to Rama. Demands grew for the mosque, a very sacred place for Muslims, to be pulled down and the temple rebuilt.

INDIA

*Troops attempt to restrain a Hindu crowd intent on destroying a mosque in Ayodhya in 1992.*

In 1992, Hindu extremists destroyed the mosque, triggering rioting and violence between Hindus and Muslims. More than 300 people died.

## RAISING THE NUCLEAR STAKES

Tensions between the two countries rose even higher in the late 1990s. In April 1998, Pakistan tested its new Ghauri nuclear missile (named after a 12th-century Muslim chief who invaded India). A month later, in retaliation, India announced that it had conducted three nuclear tests of its own. Despite calls from world leaders urging Pakistan not to reply, five further nuclear tests were carried out at the end of May. Many countries were quick to criticise these actions, and imposed economic sanctions on India and Pakistan.

**CONTINUING CONFLICT**

**October 1984** Indira Gandhi is assassinated by her bodyguards; her son, Rajiv, becomes prime minister of India

**1985** The South Asian Association for Regional Cooperation (SAARC) is launched

**December 1988** Rajiv Gandhi goes to Pakistan to attend the SAARC conference and meets Benazir Bhutto

**1989** Violence breaks out in Kashmir as militant groups demand independence; the violence continues throughout the 1990s

**1999** Pakistani forces invade Indian-held Kashmir, bringing both sides to the brink of war

**1992** Hindu extremists destroy the mosque in Ayodhya, claiming it is built on the site of the birthplace of the god, Rama

**April-May 1998** Pakistan tests its Ghauri nuclear missile; India replies with its own nuclear tests and sanctions are imposed on both countries

# STAND-OFF

**A**t the beginning of the 21st century, the issue of Kashmir remains unsolved. There are frequent exchanges of fire along the Line of Control, and Kashmir still dominates relations between India and Pakistan. It is a tragic conflict, and it will need great commitment from both sides to resolve it.

## TO THE BRINK

In December 2001, a terrorist attack on the Indian Parliament killed 14 people. India blamed Pakistan for backing the terrorists, thought to be radical Kashmiri Muslims. India closed its border with Pakistan, and both countries began to mobilise thousands of their troops. War seemed dangerously close once more.

Under pressure from the international community, the Pakistani president, Pervez Musharraf, condemned the attack. He promised to crack down on the terrorists. At the same time, though, he continued to pledge his support for the Kashmiri

*General Pervez Musharraf became leader of Pakistan in 1999.*

freedom struggle. In Kashmir, security tightened. Tension rose again in May 2002, when an attack on an army base in Indian-held Kashmir killed 30 people. Nuclear war seemed highly likely.

## RELIGIOUS HARDLINERS

The religious differences which led to the creation of modern India and Pakistan still divide them, and block a solution to the Kashmir conflict. India has a strongly pro-Hindu government, while militant groups in Kashmir hold strong Islamic views. In 2002, violent clashes between Hindus and Muslims in Gujarat, western India, left thousands of people dead. Suspicion for two massive explosions in Mumbai (Bombay) in August 2003 fell on Muslim extremists, possibly in revenge for the Gujarat killings. The tragedy is that, while many Hindus and Muslims live peacefully side by side, extremists on both sides are becoming increasingly active and dangerous.

## THE WORLD WATCHES

The international community fears that even a minor incident between India and Pakistan could trigger a nuclear war, with terrible consequences for the world. Great pressure has been put on both countries to step back from conflict and find peaceful solutions. World leaders have visited both countries to hold high-level talks. But with little sign of either country backing down, the two sides remain at a stand-off.

*Indian Prime Minister Atal Behari Vajpayee first took office in 1996. He was elected again in 1998.*

## THE FUTURE?

The future of Kashmir seems as uncertain as ever. Many solutions to the problem have been suggested. Perhaps Kashmir could become an independent state, or be permanently divided between India and Pakistan? Or perhaps the long-awaited referendum could finally be held?

In practice, nothing is possible until both sides look for compromise. For years, neither country has been prepared to make the first move, and any solution still seems a long way off. So far, all talks have led to stalemate. Kashmir remains a beautiful but bloody battleground, and its people have been torn apart by years of conflict.

Unless there is a change of heart by both India and Pakistan, the deadlock cannot be broken. Yet a solution must be found. With the added threat of nuclear war, the need for a solution is more urgent than ever.

*An Indian soldier on sentry duty near the Line of Control in Kashmir.*

**STAND-OFF**

**October 2001** The worst fighting in Kashmir for over a year breaks out when India starts shelling suspected Pakistani military positions

**December 2001** A terrorist attack on the Indian Parliament in Delhi leaves 14 people dead; Kashmiri militants are blamed

**February 2002** Hindus and Muslims clash in Gujarat, leaving thousands dead

**April-May 2002** More nuclear tests are held by both countries

**May 2002** 30 people are killed in a militant attack on an army base in Indian-held Kashmir

**August 2003** Two massive bombs explode in Mumbai; suspicion falls on Muslim extremists

**November 2003** India and Pakistan agree a ceasefire across the Line of Control in Kashmir; both sides call for peace and appear to be stepping back from the brink of war

# GLOSSARY

**Assassination** When a public or political figure is murdered, usually by a surprise attack.

**Boycott** To refuse to use or buy something.

**British Raj** The period of British rule in India. 'Raj' means 'rule'.

**Buddhism** The religion founded by the Buddha in India in the 6th century BC.

**Cabinet** A group of politicians who lead the government.

**Ceasefire** An agreement to end a war or a period of fighting.

**Charismatic** Having a very powerful or inspiring personality.

**Civil war** A war between two sides from the same country.

**Commission** A board or organisation set up by a government.

**Constitution** A written document which sets out the group of principles by which a country is governed.

**Coup** A sudden violent or illegal overthrow of an existing government.

**Crown** A ruler, such as a king or queen, and their government.

**Democracy** A government which is elected by all the people.

**Empire** A group of countries or peoples governed by a single ruler.

**Extremists** People who have very strong political or religious views.

**Fanatic** A person with extreme views or beliefs.

**Fast** To go without food or water.

**Hindus** Followers of the religion of Hinduism. In India, over three-quarters of people are Hindus.

**Jute** Fibres from the jute plant which are used to make ropes, sacks and so on.

**Line of Control** The ceasefire line between the Pakistani-held and Indian-held regions of Kashmir.

**Maharajas** Indian princes or rulers.

**Martial law** When a country is ruled by the military, instead of by a parliament.

**Massacre** When a large number of people are brutally or violently killed.

**Militant** Outspoken or even violent methods of supporting a cause.

**Missionaries** People who try to convert people of one religion to another.

**Muslims** Followers of the religion of Islam. The majority of people in Pakistan and Bangladesh are Muslims.

**Mutiny** When soldiers rebel against their officers and refuse to obey orders.

**Nationalist** Someone who is loyal or passionately devoted to their country.

**Non-alignment** A policy in which a country does not side with one particular country or interest group.

**Nuclear arms race** A struggle for power between two countries that both have nuclear weapons.

**Parliamentary** A form of government by elected representatives of the people.

**Partitioned** Divided into different parts.

**Patronage** Financial support and help given by someone, for example by a king to a favoured artist.

**Referendum** When the people of a country are asked to vote on one issue of great importance.

**Refugees** People who have fled from danger in one country to seek refuge in another, safer country.

**Republic** Country governed by an elected head of state called a president.

**Sanctions** Measures agreed by countries against another country that has broken international law.

**Satyagraha** A tactic used by Mahatma Gandhi to fight the British by peaceful means, rather than by violence. The word means 'truth force'.

**Secular** Having no connection with any particular religion.

**Sepoys** Indian soldiers who fought on behalf of the British East India Company.

**Shari'ah** Islamic law based on the Qur'an.

**Subcontinent** A large land mass that is part of a continent. The Indian subcontinent is part of Asia.

**Sultan** A Muslim ruler.

**Sultanate** A Muslim kingdom ruled by a sultan.

**Treaty** A formal agreement made between two countries.

**UN** United Nations, an international peace-keeping organisation, founded in 1945 and based in New York, USA.

**Viceroy** Someone who governs a country on behalf of another country's ruler or government.

# INDEX

INDIA